Be a Pro Seller

Be a Pro Seller

Unleash the Power of Your Sales Potential

Katerina Koehlerova

Be a Pro Seller

Unleash the Power of Your Sales Potential

Copyright © 2023 Katerina Koehlerova

All Rights Reserved

No parts of this publication may be reproduced, stored or transmitted in any form, electronic or mechanical, photocopying, recording or scanning or by any other means without the prior written permission of the copyright holder.

Katerina Koehlerova, the author of this work, has no responsibility for the persistence and accuracy of in this book provided URLs for external or third-party Internet Websites and does not guarantee that any content on such websites stays accurate. Recommendations to other websites or books should not be seen as endorsements.

ISBN: 978-1-916626-74-4

To all of you who find passion in doing what you love. Be your own success creator!

Table of Contents

About the Author i

Chapter One: Sales – From Cradle to Grave 1

Chapter Two: Sales as a Profession 14

Chapter Three: Decoding the Perfect Seller 29

Chapter Four: It's All about SALES 47

Chapter Five: Know Your Buyer 64

Chapter Six: Competition 69

Chapter Seven: You Can Do It, Provided You Want To! 85

Chapter Eight: Rise of the Phoenix – Kohli 94

Recommended Reading 104

Bibliography 106

About the Author

Katerina Köhlerova is based near London in the United Kingdom and started to work in the IT space as a sales professional late in her life. Her first job was teaching English to children in Germany. Her passion for sales brought her to the world of IT after completing her first-class degree in Modern Languages from the University of Surrey.

She has worked in the inside sales space for B2B small and medium-sized businesses for the past decade and has gathered invaluable experience through selling solutions to the DACH/ German-speaking market. Her life changed forever when she became the trusted advisor to the clients. She has helped train colleagues to excel in Consultative Selling and share her knowledge and experience with others who are passionate about starting this extremely rewarding and fulfilling journey.

Katerina's life took a turn when she was diagnosed with oral cancer in 2022 and had to undergo an operation and six weeks of daily radiotherapy. She is now in the recovery period where her body and mind have started healing. This life-changing experience has made her even more resilient and greatly focused on what she loves and is passionate about most. Life has taught her to leave out and ignore anything that does not enrich her in some way or does not provide real value. Helping others to thrive is her mission. Katerina can be reached at: www.linkedin.com/in/katerinakoehlerova

Ω

Chapter One: Sales – From Cradle to Grave

"We are all in sales."

~ Daniel Pink

Language is one of the biggest assets of the human race; social scientists even attribute the evolution of knowledge among the sapiens to their ability to communicate *more meaningfully*. Some would argue how is that possible because animals also have languages through which they convey their messages. Yes, they do; however, the difference between their languages and ours is that while they share information, we share knowledge. Imagine a monkey calling out to some of its fellow beings in the jungle. There can be only limited scenarios causing the need for this interaction; he might have found some food, seen a predator coming that way, or might be expressing anger or fondness.

There is a *definite pattern*, and apart from these *set conditions*, animals generally don't communicate what can be termed as verbal communication. However, this is not the case with humans. Our languages are complex and cover multiple subjects and types; influencing and persuading fellow men are also part of that spectrum. These two factors, my dear readers, can be described as the actual parents of sales. Influence and persuasion alter our perceptions and result in favourable or unfavourable actions towards a product, idea, service, or nation – through propaganda… it can be anything, as there are endless possibilities. This change of mind is *sales*. Ever wondered why celebrities are hired for promotional activities?

I imagine most of you recognise sales as the process in which a transaction takes place between multiple – two or more – parties, resulting in a flow of money and goods. This is what people used to think about sales until the end of the twentieth century. In today's world, the above definition covers a minuscule part of the whole process. Things have changed considerably in the last couple of decades, and now business leaders recognise

Chapter One: Sales – From Cradle to Grave

sales from the moment an impression is created till the actual transaction. It is pertinent to mention that the word transaction simply doesn't mean monetary exchange in our context. Instead, it means the desired outcome of the prior activities carried out before a transaction takes place. For example, political parties holding rallies and gatherings will be interested in winning the elections. They sell their ideas and manifesto to gain people's votes. In the *political market*, that's the sales – exchange of agenda for votes.

Now, we turn our attention towards the title of this chapter and will try to explain how every individual sells, intentionally or unintentionally, throughout their lives. I can hear some of you mumbling how is it even possible? Isn't sales for extroverts only? Those with suave looks and flashy multi-media presentations. To all of your questions, the one-word answer is NO. We all are sellers simply because that's what we all are born to do. From the day we open our eyes to this beautiful planet till our last breath, we sell, not just once but on multiple occasions and often continuously. Let's explain the concept with some real-life examples.

Scenario# 1: What do healthy infants do when they

feel hungry? Cry; why? To grab the attention of their mother (or father). Through crying, they sell their need for food. In return, their need is satisfied by feeding. This is when a seller is born in every one of us. The baby acknowledges their parents' reaction, a stimulus, to their crying and repeats it whenever they feel hungry. It is the first form of communication, and it results in a transaction, in a sale. You may be shaking your head as to how a baby's cry can be termed communication; ask any psychologist working on children's psychology, and you will understand.

Scenario# 2: You have been called by the HR department of one of the Fortune 100 companies for an interview. What will you do? Apart from researching about the company and the job, you will go through your CV to prepare well for the questions to get the desired position. Why are you preparing so hard? Because you want to improve upon the already favourable perception the company's management has about you. In business terminology, you intend to sell your skills to the prospective buyer. In this scenario, if the company is impressed with you and offers you the job. There you have the desired outcome: this is the close of the transaction, another sale.

Scenario# 3: It is the last day of your university; all your classmates are embracing each other and exchanging numbers to remain in contact. From the corner of your eye, you see the person of your dreams. Acknowledging this might be the last chance you will meet him/her any time soon, you approach the person and confess your love, informing him/her about your feelings and promise to keep him/her happy if he/she accepts you as a partner. In our parlance, that's your sales pitch, and if the chosen person accepts you, voila, we have a sale.

These are but some of the selling examples from our daily lives. You have to understand that sales as a process is driven by human psychology. The moment buyers feel that they are getting more value than the asking price, a cost-benefit analysis of sorts, they will purchase the offering. This may include your skills, love, or simply any tangible product. Selling, and conversely buying, is entrenched in our nature, something which we can't live without. It doesn't matter whether you are an introvert or an extrovert, a partygoer or a lone ranger; it comes naturally to all of us, as demonstrated by the above examples.

In one of his books, *To Sell is Human*, Daniel Pink – an NYT best-selling author – describes how eighty per cent of our interactions amount to *non-selling sales* – a term he devised to define activities that persuade and influence others. Have you ever tried out a brand after hearing good about it from someone you know? Sounds familiar; this is non-selling sales, and it is happening all around us.

Though word-of-mouth influence has been a proven fact, its importance has increased with the proliferation of products, the advent of online buying behaviour, and social media. While shopping, we all have a preferred list of brands either because of our prior experience or because someone we know recommended it. That recommendation is word-of-mouth which has created a positive image, coaxing you to buy the product. The whole process constitutes sales, with the *influencer* being the non-selling agent since, most probably, they won't be getting any benefits for the purchase of the products. Then why did they praise the product in the first instance? Because of a man's inherent desire to influence and persuade fellow beings. After monetary reward, appreciation and respect rank highly on our list of desires.

Chapter One: Sales – From Cradle to Grave

Have you considered why social media has been such a big factor in our lives? A general reply would be that it has removed the communication barriers, and people can now interact easily while thousands of miles apart. That's right, and there is no denying this fact. However, the more appropriate reply would be that it has allowed us to get instant *acknowledgement*. As soon as you post a check-in on Facebook or any other social media platform, you will get bombarded with messages from your friends, relatives, and peers asking for reviews and recommendations. Replying to them with your feedback brings you personal satisfaction, which, honestly speaking, we all crave. Deep inside, one feels like providing useful information that can impact readers' lives. Again, there is nothing wrong with it because that's a part of our nature. On second thought, it is our nature. Our priorities may change, for example, a foodie may want to be acknowledged as a food expert, while for a bookworm, being recognised as a book expert will be high on the list; the desire to influence and persuade remains the same. We do not need to be experts in those fields but a few steps ahead of our readers.

Thus, my friends, we all are into sales. We either do it professionally and make a living out of it or do it for personal satisfaction. Whatever the reason, the benefits to be accrued while doing so are extremely rewarding. This brings us to a vital question; if every individual is inherently a salesperson, why do most fail when pursuing their career in the field?

Stumbling Blocks – Why People Falter?

The reason behind writing this book is to provide a guide about making a successful career in sales to professionals and aspirants. It is not an academic book that will provide its readers with different selling theories developed over time. Instead, I will share my decade-long experience in the field to appraise you about sales' DOs and DON'Ts, especially in the changing scenario of developments in the field of Information Technology. Information plays a critical role in sales, and the rule is simple: a buyer will not purchase your product/solution if they don't know it. However, what kind of information needs to be shared and who is your ideal customer/client remains equally important. This is where often sales and marketing people are at odds with each other.

Based on my personal experience, people fail to make

a good and prosperous career in sales due to several reasons; not carrying out enough research to know about their customers, not being able to build a rapport with their potential clients, not being confident about the product themselves, applying similar practices or techniques in different markets and industries, not paying attention to market trends and competitors, not being able to look at the bigger picture, and over-reliance on brand value.

These are the most common mistakes committed by individuals or even teams, which lead to sales decline and hence cost them their jobs. It is very much possible that within some organisations, multiple factors exist as a combination. However, this is not an exhaustive list, there are other factors, and we will discuss them as we move along. While the following chapters constitute the details of all these and other factors and personal recommendations for rectifications, it is imperative to deliberate upon them so that you may know how people falter to make use of their inherent talent.

The most common cause of not being able to convert a lead into sales is the seller's inability to know about the true needs of their customers. This generally happens more in industrial sales than consumer sales (details about the terms in later chapters). As a seller, our first priority should be to ascertain the need of the customers. Though when dealing with corporate clients, one often gets a detailed Request for Quotation (RFQ), sometimes called an inquiry; there are chances that the buyer might not be aware of the actual product themselves. How is it possible? In most cases, a buyer is not a technical person and simply forwards whatever demand has been generated by the production department. This is why I cannot stress enough that it is imperative for the sales guy to thoroughly research the client and then submit their quotations. They may also pay a visit to the buyer for more information for clarification. Similarly, when selling to a company, you need to know about its hierarchy and be able to communicate with the respective buying influencers within the company.

When I started as a sales rep, my seniors told me a cardinal rule – sell the product to yourself before selling it to a stranger. What does it mean? Have a thorough understanding of the product, and learn its pros and cons. Then put yourself in your customer's shoes and sell the solution to yourself with all honesty. If you can achieve this task, rest assured you can sell it to anyone because then you will know a) all the attributes of your product and b) can plan out beforehand the questions a buyer might be asking when you approach them. However, this is one practice that is being overlooked often, especially by young professionals. As mentioned before, sales is all about playing with human psychology; the more one feels confident about their product, the better.

Another one of those common practices, which, despite being highlighted, is often followed by the sellers. There is no one-fits-all solution in sales because you are interacting with different individuals having diverse requirements. Treating them all as similar is considered a sin by sales gurus. The problem stems from the fact that salespersons don't think about whom they are selling to and only concentrate on their product.

You often hear about thinking out of the box and developing new strategies to increase revenue in your management and marketing classes, as business students, and even during meetings, as professionals. All these are good because without evolving, a company, and an individual, can't survive – the biggest example being Nokia – however, one can't totally deny the data. You must strategise and plan according to market trends, including customer preferences and your competitors' products. It allows you and your company to know where they can place their product/solution in the market.

The marketing department of a company enlightens the customers about the company and its products. They create brand awareness among their targeted audience/potential prospects, which should result in the generation of higher quality leads which are handled warm by the sales team and should result in sales. Therefore, be bold but not disrespectful in sharing your feedback and market experiences. Never shy away from that because it will serve marketing guys and the company a world of good. Though sales teams can't directly impact the product/ solution improvement procedure, their first-hand data can assist product management to understand in more detail the needs of the customers, which can pave the way for future changes, improvements, and product enhancements.

Above is the synopsis of what we will be discussing in this book later on, so don't sweat over it. I will explain the problems and will try to present the solutions based on my professional experience while working and interacting with successful sales professionals.

Having said that, all is not doom and gloom. You all have what it takes to be successful and make a prosperous career in the field. As long as there is humanity, there will be a need for great salespeople. However, one needs to align themselves with the rules and practices to flourish. Remember, work smartly; there is no need to reinvent the wheel, just tweak or modify it to your requirements. Too often, in order to make a mark, people lose the plot and achieve nothing or get sidetracked, and potential achievement comes to nothing. Time is a precious resource, don't waste it on futile activities. Learn to analyse and plan while keep updating your skillset continuously. And, if you don't know how to do that, this book is just for you. Happy reading!

Ω

Chapter Two: Sales as a Profession

In the United Kingdom, on average, every fifteenth person is associated with sales or a related profession[1]. This is after the financial meltdown at the turn of the millennium and the COVID-19 pandemic. If you are wondering the figures are unusually high for the country, you will be surprised to know that the pattern prevails in most developed countries. Therefore, sales, being one of the highest sought-after fields, is a global phenomenon. So, what makes the profession tick? And why are people drawn to it?

There are many reasons behind the higher percentage of professionals opting for sales, but the two most prominent are – higher rewards associated with

---

[1] A report issued by the UK government, titled Employment by Occupation: https://www.ethnicity-facts-figures.service.gov.uk/work-pay-and-benefits/employment/employment-by-occupation/latest#download-the-data

the job and relatively less technical expertise required. While hiring a sales professional, employers usually consider the aptitude and personality of the candidates rather than technical or academic expertise. Those with strong and interesting personal character, having excellent communication skills are generally preferred. However, there is a downside; with companies relying on aptitude and skill-assessment tests without having quantifiable recruitment criteria, the chances of employing unsuitable candidates are relatively high compared to other departments. The human factor involved in the decision-making is what makes sales fascinating, though sometimes it can be cumbersome.

Later in the book, we will explain how to ace the deal as a sales professional and enjoy the perks that come along. In this chapter, however, we will discuss the profession, its demands, and how it can help fast-track an individual's professional growth.

The Real Deal

The primary goal of every existing commercial enterprise is to make profits. No business person starts a new venture without being driven by an outcome called problem-solving for customers, which leads to profit. Regarding philanthropy, there are non-profit organisations that rely on donations and aid; that's another topic outside the scope of this book. Ask any entrepreneur, young or old, what they want in return for investing a large sum in an enterprise; answer will be similar, more money which translates into greater profit and return on investment.

In other words, if making profits is the sole reason to exist, management will require a workforce that can engage prospective buyers and who can bring value to the table so that the customer is convinced that your solution will solve his problem. The necessity to sell gives birth to a sales team to grow the company's revenue. Simply put, organisations can't live without sales, just like humans, in general, can't live without selling to one another. With so much at stake, it is only natural that the focus will be greater on performance, where higher rewards serve primarily as the added incentive.

Humans, by nature, are driven by emotions as buyers. We want more value for every penny spent. Hence, we will buy the product we perceive as more beneficial while neglecting the other. It requires patience, self-control, fortitude, and great communication skills to reply to all queries and present the items as the best possible solution.

Over the years, companies have developed sales tools that incorporate buyer preferences, product types, market trends, and competitors to provide useful information, which goes a long way in developing a comprehensive sales strategy that can yield results in years to come. Marketing, especially advertising, has improved by leaps and bounds in the last five decades, providing sellers with a headstart to close the deal. Though sales professionals and marketers are usually at loggerheads, both know that they are indispensable to each other.

So, while it can be said that along with other fields, sales have also inculcated automation to make informed decisions, one must always be wary of the fallout. In sales, one can't be 100% sure if the trend will remain the same because of the human desire to change. Sometimes this happens even in corporate selling. My advice to all experienced or novice professionals is never to completely rely on past data; take it as a guide only. Yes, it can give you trends and helps strategise, but it can't predict an outcome with 100% certainty. Always be prepared to expect the unexpected and be open to making decisions based on intuition; gut feeling usually guides a person to the better option when no significant information is available.

Sales Process

I know there is too much content available on the topic on the internet; however, I have observed that the majority is too bookish and hence carries little weight for any sales practitioner. This is why, I have designed my sales process in line with current scenarios and practices so that our readers can relate to all the steps.

Lead Generation → Initial Sales Call → RFQs/EoI → Sales Quote → Sales → After Sales Support/Follow-up

Above are my six steps that define sales, and though they may vary according to product type and market, most are applicable. Sometimes you will find a couple of them merged into one or a change in order; the essence will remain the same.

Chapter Two: Sales as a Profession

Lead Generation

This is the result of all the marketing efforts, either traditional or digital, undertaken by a company. If you are wondering what lead generation is, it can be defined as attracting prospective customers to your solution that can resolve their problem and bring the customer a tangible return on investment in the future. At this stage, they will contact you, enquire about your product, and leave. Now, please deliberate very carefully over the words.

First, I have used the term prospective customer because, at the moment, we are not sure whether they will actually buy our product or not; not every lead generates sales. They have heard about our product through a source, which can be either a media campaign, word-of-mouth, search engine, or website visit, and are willing to consider it provided the product or solution ticks nearly all the boxes. In simpler terms, lead generation is the stage where the customer is searching for a solution to their problem and comes across your product to ascertain whether the solution could be the answer to their problem. Then they need to establish if they want to find out more. Have you ever visited any website which asks for your details to access the information? That's lead generation for the company. Your provided information acts as a point of contact, allowing a sales representative to make a sales call.

Most of you may be thinking, what's such a big deal in that? A random guy comes in, asks about our product, and leaves; what significance does the process have? My dear readers, I will advise you to come out of that mindset. Any interaction with a prospective buyer should be valued. Think from their point of view; they must have reached out to you after hearing something good or genuinely feeling your product can satisfy their needs. There is a positive perception, but the customer needs to do due diligence to determine if the solution is the right fit for them to resolve their burning pain point.

Initial Sales Call

Lead generation provides an opening you, as a seller, have to capitalise upon through an effective and meaningful initial sales call - the second step. This is the most important step of the entire cycle. Ask any senior sales expert, and they will inform you a customer is gained or lost here. If you can impress the enquirer by presenting yourself as a trustworthy and dependable supplier, then, in most likelihood, you will be able to secure the deal.

However, that can only be achieved once you have their confidence, and a great sales call goes a long way in building that long-lasting relationship. A couple of tips for young practitioners; listen carefully and try to grasp maximum information from the buyers, and don't bombard them with excessive details. They can be shared at the time of a technical/demo call where implementation needs and other questions are discussed. For starters, share only relevant information to help them figure out the benefits your product holds for them; more on that in the next chapters.

It is important to note that business deals are not done in one sitting; multiple meetings take place in which both parties negotiate, trying to arrive at an understanding acceptable to all. So, don't try to hasten the process; instead, try to learn more about the customer you are dealing with to present relevant information.

RFQ/EoI

Assuming you were able to win over your audience during the initial sales call or presentation, the purchaser will formally ask you to submit your quotation mentioning product details, price, delivery terms, and lead time. There are numerous names for the process Request for Quotation (RFQ), Expression of Interest (EoI), Demand, or Enquiry.

The Sales Quote

Don't get confused with the choice of words used by the purchaser; concentrate on the most important document you have to prepare as a salesperson – the sales quotation. It should include all the details, so there is no ambiguity at the time of the transaction. If you are selling a technical product, mention all the relevant features while avoiding vague terms that may confuse the buyer. The best way of preparing a sales quote is to mention the details which you had shared with them in your earlier conversations or presentations. It will reaffirm the notion that you are a genuine company which delivers on its promises, nothing more and nothing less.

Chapter Two: Sales as a Profession

Sales

Acceptance of your quotation will result in the issuance of a purchase order, asking you to deliver the items at the agreed-upon terms and conditions. The Purchase order, or PO, is a legal binding document where the customer has confirmed the intent to buy.

After-Sales Support

Numerous research has shown that the cost of retaining a customer is far less than acquiring a new one. Therefore, after-sales support becomes a major part of the overall sales process, especially when dealing with corporate clients. Always make sure to touch upon your customers after a successful sale, and ask for their feedback; it will initiate a longstanding and desired relationship.

Selling Tangible vs. Intangible Goods

In the second half of the twentieth century, as developed countries shifted from a manufacturing-based economy to a service-based economy, a new terminology gained prominence *Intangible Goods*. They are the services offered to provide a better and enhanced experience. Though these goods don't exist as a product/item which can be preserved or physically examined, they are the value-added benefits to ensure excellent customer interaction. Counselling and consultation are examples of intangible goods readily offered.

Since service-providing companies have no tangible item to show to back their claims, they have to plan their sales strategy around extra benefits their customers may accrue while availing them. Another important aspect is to treat every individual differently and offer maximum customization to make consumers feel privileged and special. Remember, word-of-mouth plays a significant role in the promotion of a service provider. Consequently, excellent customer service is a must for companies selling intangible goods.

Types of Sales

With the change in customer preferences and management practices over a period of time, sales have also evolved considerably. Initially starting from direct sales, where manufacturers used to sell directly to the end consumers, the field has grown into different types suitable for specific products.

B2C

Short form for Business-to-Costumer, a sale is classified as a B2C if the business is selling the product to the consumer. Intermediaries like retail outlets and superstores are prime examples of B2C sales. This type of sale is very flexible in nature, involves fast-moving consumer goods (FMCG), and doesn't usually conform to the sales process mentioned earlier. Another important feature is that the purchase behaviour of the buyers is impromptu and thus should be monitored constantly.

B2B

Business-to-Business, B2B, is a sale between two companies. However, there are further divisions within this classification.

- Customers using other companies' finished products to produce their products, like Toyota buying metallic sheets from local vendors to assemble its cars.

- Customers buying products from manufacturers for reselling purposes, like Walmart and Tesco, who buy in bulk quantities from respective manufacturing companies and then sell the items to their end users.

B2B sales are driven by rational decision-making after rigorous negotiations and, at times, customization. Since sellers and buyers are commercial entities, it is also known as Industrial Sales.

Consultative

A relatively new type developed over the turn of the century, consultative sales allow customers to share their needs and then propose a suitable solution. More and more companies are now inclined to go the consultative route of selling as they are selling a solution to a customer problem and not a product that consists of features only. Sellers take on an advisory role, enlightening the buyer about the available options based on their needs and queries. A car showroom selling an assortment of models and brands is an example of consultative sales. The sales rep would recommend the most appropriate item after listening to their customer's budget and requirements.

Online Sales

Online sales are when customers order their products online without physical examination trusting the website's reputation to ensure the delivery of quality products. The biggest and most prominent example is Amazon, which acts as a marketplace for manufacturers and buyers to meet and undertake commercial activities.

What Lies Ahead?

With the advancements in the field of Information Technology, there were concerns regarding the existence of the previously most in-demand profession. As companies tried to reach out to their end consumers, some industry experts believed that days for a sales field force were numbered. They argued that it would not take companies long to reduce their seller count, increasing their reliance on marketing for revenue generation. However, we have witnessed the opposite, and the profession is on a resurgence trail. Instead, the factors that were supposed to overtake the sales force are helping them grow. The most prominent examples are Amazon and other online selling platforms.

As the world embraced the novel concept of online shopping during the last decade of the twentieth century, experts started predicting the downfall of prevailing physical, person-to-person selling practices. They opined that companies should maximise their revenues through extensive marketing campaigns and making the products available online. They argued that having a formal sales force would only burden the company financially; hence, it should be outsourced to third parties, just like production was outsourced to countries with cheap labour like China. However, these factors have only helped to enhance the importance of having an excellent sales field.

Ω

Chapter Three: Decoding the Perfect Seller

After briefly describing the term sales, its types, and processes, let's move towards the book's main topic—how to build a successful career in sales, and what skills and traits will be required to achieve that goal. Yes, you require both to reach the top, apart from the hard work.

Just a little clarification; while many people use the words skills and traits interchangeably, they are different. Skills refer to qualities one acquires through learning, whereas traits are characteristics a person is born with and only needs to polish them for maximum utilisation. Since football fever is on, I am writing this as the FIFA world cup 2022 is in full flow in Qatar, let's take Messi and Ronaldo's example. Both are great players, one of a kind. Hence, there has been a raging debate for more than a decade as to who is better.

Ronaldo, or CR7 as his fans affectionately call him, is all about hard work, endurance, and discipline. Looking at him, one feels as if he is a machine, a goal-scoring machine. Over the years, we have heard from his teammates about his strict work ethic and how religiously he follows his routine without any letup. Furthermore, he upgraded his skillset and evolved into a world-class striker from a winger who can score from any angle and range. This has allowed him to rule major football leagues across Europe and has provided longevity to his career.

Messi, on the other hand, is so natural and has a wonderful flow to his gameplay. Even if someone doesn't like football, they will still want to see Messi play. He is poetry in motion. Playing football comes naturally to him; hence, his style of playing is more free-flowing and pleasing to the eye. Now it doesn't mean that Messi doesn't have to work hard; certainly, he has to. Remember, he is not as physically gifted as his counterpart. As a result, his biggest challenge was to work on his fitness. Otherwise, he wouldn't have been able to compete with the demands of the game and hence, would have failed to realise his full potential.

Just like having an abundance of natural talent is not enough for Messi to become the best player, similarly, being born with requisite traits is not enough to be a good salesperson. One must put in the hard yards to maximise the gains. Conversely, even if a person is not born with the expertise, they can still excel and reach the top, provided they are willing to learn new skills and work hard like Ronaldo.

Disclaimer: the above debate is not to argue who is the better player; it was just to show how one can achieve greatness in their field. Though I like Messi more, then again, you must have guessed it ☺

Similarly, for professionals, young and old, either aspiring to make a name for themselves in sales or are already plying their trade, it is important to first analyse themselves, identify their strengths and weaknesses, and then plan accordingly. We all are accustomed to performing SWOT analysis; sales and marketing guys do it for products to gauge their feasibility, while business students do it for studying commercial organisations. However, it is imperative for any individual to first apply the same rules upon themselves to ascertain their actual self. Based on the evaluation, we can identify and/or recognise our true potential, and, consequently, can build upon our strengths and eliminate our weaknesses.

As we have mentioned before, there are different types of sales, and they all require separate qualities. So, it is essential for a person to find a fit between their personality and the requirements. Don't follow others who have been successful over the years blindly while making a choice; otherwise, the decision will come back to haunt you in the long run. One important note; while examining yourself, remain impartial and avoid all biases. They can affect the results big time.

To further clarify the difference between traits and skills, we will discuss them in detail below:

Essential Traits for a Seller

Most of the outsiders, those who are not working in sales, consider us all to be similar. For them, we possess the same qualities and characteristics; nothing can be far from reality than this (stereotypical view). Yes, we do share some traits, but it happens in every profession. Research shows at least four types of sellers exist, and all of them have been successful; one can't be classified as superior or better than the others (Alfred, 2020), (Freedman, 2023).

We have said it before and are reiterating the same point that, as a salesperson, we deal with human beings. It has been a proven fact that no two individuals act the same way. Psychology says that despite being presented with similar situations and problems, people react differently and, more often than not, arrive at the same conclusion by taking separate routes. I am not a mathematician, but I know for sure that a mathematical problem can be solved using different methods, and they all will be considered correct unless, of course, the tutor has specified a specific method. Now imagine solving a complex equation like a human being. There can't be one simple correct method!

Surprisingly, though, even experienced sales professionals fail to grasp this fact. In my professional career, I have met many people complaining about not being able to close the deal despite offering the best prices. My friends, we have to acknowledge that price is not just the sole criterion to persuade buyers. Yes, it plays a big role but not every time. Purchasers often look for intangible benefits like being trustworthy, perceived quality of the product/solution, nature of the support services being offered in the Sales Level Agreement (SLA), and more likely involvement with technical support which should be on the highest level before approving your quotation. Thus, never look for a one-fit-all formula because that will not work; not every time, that is.

Since there is no cheat code in sales and separate *formulas* can be used to *crack an equation*, salespersons have been known to employ different proven techniques to achieve their desired results. These techniques, over the years, become a part of their personalities, which the researchers and top management have defined under four types. They are:

Bold

They are the typical salesperson type usually associated with someone who is willing to take the bull by its horn and tame it. Some of the characteristics this type possesses are; assertiveness, competitiveness, impulsive decision-making (this can also be their negative attribute), dominating, intuitive, and readiness to go the extra mile.

Listener

As the name suggests, this type of salesperson pays more attention to knowing more about the needs of the customers rather than dictating them. They ask questions and listen carefully to fully understand their buyers' actual requirements. Thus, they are calmer, friendlier, more patient, and place a high value on a good relationship with the customers. Their theory is to create long-lasting trust with the customers and not settle for short-term gains.

Problem Solver

They are the tech guys, always ready with their electronic gadgets to present, churning out data at will to validate their decisions. Such salespersons are very analytical, fact-based, system-oriented, and formal – everything needs to be done in a certain manner. They believe in short and meaningful conversations and are solution-oriented and serious. On a lighter note, often, they are the blue-eyed boys of their managers.

Eloquent

The talkative guy or the chatterbox, such salespersons love conversing, are very creative, informal, always seem to know everything, enthusiastic, easy-going, loyal, but more importantly, know how to please other people. However, their strength can turn into a weakness since they like to talk themselves, which may put off some customers. With them, one never feels bored; their spontaneous personality makes up for what they lack in analytical thinking.

This shows how different personalities can work together in a department to achieve common goals. Without undermining other professions, in my knowledge based on my experience and observations, sales is the only field that allows such diversity.

Regardless of the personality-type, certain traits are a must for a long and successful career in sales. Below are seven important traits I believe are important for any individual to succeed in sales. Obviously, the list is not exhaustive, and additions can be made.

Positivity & Hunger to Succeed

If you are a seller, optimism should be the characteristic others should see in you. There should be an inner drive to be able to make a difference despite all the odds. One needs to remain hopeful all the time and anticipate good news. In case of a rejection, take it on the chin, and look for the mistakes to perform better next time. A salesperson should always maintain a positive outlook, no matter the circumstances and situation.

Confidence

As stated in the earlier chapter, human buying habit differ considerably, from being impulsive and emotional to research-oriented and detailed. Thus, it takes guts and lots of confidence in one's abilities while trying to sell. The inherent belief *I can do it* is the cornerstone of a seller's success. Another important factor is sellers' confidence in their products. They should be hundred per cent sure that, given the specifications and qualities, their brand is the best possible solution for the customers, addressing their needs.

Flexibility

A good salesperson is flexible enough to find his way out of problems; they should show resilience in the face of risk. One can plan as much as they want, all the bases can't be covered all the time. Therefore, when an unexpected situation arises, the person should be able to navigate it. Overcoming several objections provides valuable experience to sellers when they negotiate with their customers. It affords them an insight that can see through buyers' needs.

Honesty

One thing that is essential for any company is repeat orders, which can only happen when buyers view the organisation as trustworthy and reliant. Studies show that the cost of finding a new customer is double that of retaining one (Kingwill, 2015). In order to build a long relationship, sellers need to be honest with their customers. Overpromising and making false promises at the time of sales will dishearten the buyer and cause them to bad mouth the product and the company, something no one can afford in this competitive and information-driven world. It is often said, *better to lose a deal than integrity and reputation.*

Chapter Three: Decoding the Perfect Seller

Persistence

Nothing comes easy in this life, more so if you are into sales. The ability to keep knocking on the door, no matter what is what separates a successful seller from others. Once you have set your target, persist with it regardless of the situation and obstacles. *The word failure should not exist in your dictionary; either you achieve your goal or learn from your errors.* With this mindset only you will find the motivation to go out and meet the customers despite their rejections. In sales, the rule is, don't expect positive results but plan as if you have already secured the deal.

Determination

By determined, I mean remaining focused and not paying attention to distractions like naysayers and office politics. One should only concentrate on their goals and means to achieve them. There is a quote attributed to Winston Churchill, "You will never reach your destination if you stop and throw stones at every dog that barks."

That's what salespersons need to do; keep your ears and eyes open, but don't let the noise get to your head.

Your target should always remain the priority; even if you have achieved it, plan ahead for the upcoming events.

Consulting

This is the evolution of a salesperson in the twenty-first century; I believe in moving forward, it will be an important trait for a sales professional. With technological advancements and the instant availability of information, customers have become well-informed. Hence, the role of a seller is to act as a consultant who guides their buyers and assists them in finding the right product or solution. The trait is more applicable when selling services, which are intangible in nature and customers will require more information before signing up for any additional services, but one can't discount its importance in product sales as well.

Essential Skills for a Seller

Skills are something a person learns and develops over a period of time. Unlike traits, they can be acquired and mastered through practice, experience, or traditional learning. The most prominent example of a skill is communication skill; people who are not naturally gifted communicators can also learn it and be good at it. There are different kinds of skills; some are common, such as interpersonal skills, while others are specific, for example, programming skills which will only help you if you intend to become a software programmer.

Like other professions, natural talent is not enough in sales; skills are also important. They allow sellers to remain updated with the ongoing trends and perform their duties well. Some of the most relevant and vital skills for salespersons are (Bariuad, 2022), (Kwapong):

Develop Entrepreneurial Mindset

For the outside world, sellers represent the company and should take full ownership of the product. Understanding the formalities of running a business allows them to strategise effectively when negotiating with their customers, especially corporate clients. It can help them present an ideal solution, more suitable to the users' needs and in line with their industrial trends. Sellers with an entrepreneurial mindset can take on an advisory role better, helping customers make informed decisions.

Effective Communication

Salespersons need to have excellent communication skills not only to deal with their customers but also for an effective and timely interdepartmental flow of information. Keeping organisational peers updated with the plans allows the process to function smoothly, without any hiccups, which more often than not results in enhanced customer satisfaction. Short, crisp, and precise instructions, either written or verbal, go a long way in avoiding undue misunderstanding.

Similarly, while communicating with clients, all the details should be presented clearly in no uncertain terms so that there remains no ambiguity in the minds of the buyers, which may cause inconvenience later on, with the possibility of harming the relationship altogether.

Be a Good Listener

One of the biggest myths regarding salespersons is that they only like to talk and don't listen much. To some extent, this may well be true; however, that's the wrong approach. A seller should be a good listener and a great observer. Humans communicate more with their bodies, non-verbal communication - gestures and expressions, than words, and sellers would do well to note them to ascertain what their customers are thinking and want. It will allow them to gain the trust of their clients and to build up a great rapport with their audience once it is their turn to speak.

Interrupting the buyers regularly or bombarding them with excessive information will make them not only disinterested but also frustrated in the communication, resulting in losing the order.

Negotiation

A deal usually doesn't close in one go; both parties negotiate vigorously to accrue maximum benefits for their respective companies. Sellers, thus, should be well-versed in negotiating techniques so that they may drive home their point of view without sounding arrogant and aggressive. The aim should be to arrive at a win-win situation, which can pave the way for future deals.

Excellent negotiation skills are of utmost importance for industrial sellers (B2B selling), where several meetings take place, even by the legal teams, to contemplate the clauses and conditions before either party agrees to sign the dotted line.

Relationship Building

Retaining a customer has always been the primary concern for any organisation. It is cost-effective than searching for new customers every time. Repeat customers are the backbone of the business as these customers generate revenue year on year. This allows sales teams to focus on new customers/ net new logos whilst renewal teams take care of customer renewals and any additional post-sales needs regarding purchased support and services. Therefore, relationship building is a skill sellers should master if they want to attain the top position in this profession. Always honour and respect your client and make them feel in great and capable hands by going the extra mile for them.

Problem-Solving

In the modern world of social media and cut-throat competition, this skill, in my opinion, ranks among the top three most essential ones. When a prospective customer approaches a seller, he expects the other person to understand their problem and proposes an appropriate solution. This means every salesperson should be well-versed in deciphering the message upon receipt and make sure that their reply addresses the core need. In such a situation, they need to take a consultative role, educate the buyer about what the solution to their problem may be, and, in the end, propose a product/solution.

However, generally opposite happens. Habitually, sellers try to force down their brand without even realizing whether it's a good fit. Consequently, many buyers leave unsatisfied, never to return.

Time Management

Time is one resource we all waste carelessly without realizing its importance. For sellers, effective and efficient time management is a must; there are no two ways about it. Prioritise your tasks and try to complete them within the stipulated time. Spending more time on one activity will reduce the margin for the other, which will start a chain reaction resulting in delayed responses and annoyed customers.

Sales is not complicated. However, as sellers we need to understand the scope of our role, collaboration, utilisation of tools and knowledge base, to understand the given options and also consider any limitations.

Moreover, having said that, one can't remain idle and let their competitors move forward. There is a very fine line between being proactive and being careless. If you know the difference between the two, no one can stop your ascent to the top.

Ω

Chapter Four: It's All about SALES

Let's get down to the business end!

We have discussed at length the essentials required for making a successful career in sales. Now, we will talk about putting all of those into practice. What needs to happen in order to produce positive results, not just for a season or one quarter but continuously for a long period of time you will see in this chapter. You can say that this chapter is all about the DOs and DON'Ts of sales and how to train oneself to master the process.

A word of caution: top management wants sales as it leads to growth and a greater revenue. Your manager may support you for a quarter or two despite not meeting the targets, keeping your professional growth in mind. However, the progress should translate into figures soon; otherwise, you know *what's gonna happen...!* The idea is not to scare anyone but to show the true picture.

For many, the high-risk, high-reward nature of a sales job doesn't guarantee enough job security since the proverbial sword of Damocles is always hanging over one's head, causing anxiety and uneasiness. For others like me, that's the exciting part. From a personal point of view, I can safely say the competitive nature of a sales job keeps me going. It acts as a motivation to get up early in the morning for work. Nothing against those who like *to play safe*, but isn't monotony boring?

I guess it has to do with the mindset; yes, it is all about the mindset. Recall in the last chapter how we stressed the importance of the right attitude. Sales is all about being mentally strong and possessing the right attitude to defeat all the negativity. You have competition all around. Other companies are trying to access your customers while fellow team members are putting in their (extra) effort to get the management's nod, and naysayers are gossiping behind your back. When everyone is busy trying to keep you down (figuratively speaking), soar high into the skies like an eagle, enchanting and mesmerising everyone all along. Simply tune into your inner self and use the powers within you to cut out the white noise around you. Allow yourself to steer towards your goals. "To succeed" means different things to different people. If you succeed in sales what will be your next challenge? Only you know the value of yourself and how much this value will translate into monetary and other rewards. Enjoy equally both the journey and the end goal! Repeat to yourself daily: I am the best sales person, they will ever meet! I never feel like losing customers as I attract the right people. I am creating abundance in my life. My friends, it will not be an easy flight, but it will be an enjoyable and highly adventurous one; I guarantee you that.

You might be thinking excitement is getting the better of Katerina. Well, that's how it should be. One should be excited talking about their profession, especially in sales, where there is so much to learn, observe, and experience. Ever wonder why top salespersons are also good storytellers? Because of their journey. I have been in sales for almost a decade now, and I believe I can tell a different story every day for at least a year; think about those who have spent more time on their sales journey.

The idea behind sharing my thoughts is to encourage and inspire you to think positively and always view the glass as half full (remember the last chapter?). Psychologists believe that individuals are moved more if personal and factual experiences are shared with them than fictional stories. Those who are into cricket know that last year (I am still in 2022), during the Ashes series, the English team came under severe criticism. They were not performing well and looked short of ideas. The cricket board decided to change the management, captain and coach, and since then, we all know the results.

Players have remained the same; rules have not changed, so why such a drastic turn of events? All because of the mindset. Both Stokes and McCullum decided not to go down without putting up a fight. And boy, have they delivered... The cricketing world has been taken by surprise, and a new term has been coined to match the style of play, *Bazball*. Talk about a dramatic turnaround in months. That's something we watch in movies, but they have done it in real life. The team is oozing with confidence, and all the experts are backing England to thrash Australia come next summer. How was all this possible? Mental toughness and positivity. There will be days when the English team will not perform, but then the failure will be termed an aberration and not normalcy.

I have always believed that a salesperson should follow sports, especially team sports like football (soccer for our American friends), cricket, rugby, etc. Confused? We can pick many things from them. How? Take Bazball, for example; fearlessness, team spirit, great amount of practice and consistency, motivation, and self-confidence, shown by the English cricket team, are very useful for us. More importantly, the way a team makes a comeback from a seemingly impossible situation can be used as a reference point to overcome our personal adversities. Lastly, sports also provide an outlet for sales professionals to vent out their frustrations and anger and refocus on the job at hand. In real life, nothing happens on its own; one must make it happen. Yes, luck may play a part, but we can't count on it all the time. And most of the time, an individual must make their own luck. Just like the English cricket team, their recent red-ball success is due to their fearless attitude. They wanted to make things happen, and hence, the results have gone their way.

For us in sales, applicable techniques are not different from sports people. Like them, we are also in the limelight; thus, our *fall* also gets highlighted and discussed more. As soon as there is a dip in sales, everyone will start talking, oblivious to the complex nature of our job. Calling on customers with varying personalities and needs and trying to meet their expectations every time is indeed challenging. It can take a lot out of you mentally and physically. Yet think about the satisfaction when they acknowledge your efforts and the appreciation your manager showers upon you in front of your peers. Isn't it worth it…? Yes, in other departments certainly, one gets appreciated and acknowledged as well, but in sales, you have the figures to show for it and it happens more frequently. It is worth mentioning that some companies for each great small, medium, or large win let you ring the bell in the sales department/ usually open plan office. So that the whole team can join in on a quick celebration and acknowledge the success. The win is being shared, which is a highly inspirational and energising feeling for the team. Remember: Celebrate your wins and learn from your temporary setbacks!

The whole build-up is to motivate you to look into the eyes of upcoming challenges and say *I am ready*. Believe me, you will need this attitude. However, don't do it without adequate preparations; that would be a proverbial suicide, not self-confidence.

Approach of Successful Sellers

Enough of the motivational speaking; let's deliberate on the approach or the tactics. Like everything in life, the correct approach towards executing a sales plan is of utmost importance for any professional. Well, it is a no-brainer really, still, some people fail to acknowledge its significance. You simply can't just walk into the office and decide, *well, this is how I am gonna do it...* It's not on! There should be a method behind your execution of a plan. One can't shoot an arrow in the air and hope it will find the target. *Seriously!*

Sell Your Product to Yourself First

If you recall, I briefly touched upon this in the first chapter when discussing why people usually fail in this profession. Now is the time to dwell on it a bit more.

Try asking any seller about their (honest) opinion regarding the product/solution they are selling. Immediately, they will retort; *we have the best product; it can do this, do that, and is the answer to all your problems. Use it, and you will have no worries at all...* Till this part, I have no issues. I strongly believe a seller should hold a strong and favourable bias for the product/solution they are selling. Otherwise, how will you sell it? Try thinking about; how it will feel if a seller admits in front of their customer that their product is good, but the competitor's is the best. Instantly, the reply will be, *thank you for coming; I will buy that one then.*

Hold on; I know what you guys are thinking. In this day and age, a product/solution is not just the item/services a customer uses; it refers to the whole experience. It is very much possible that the best quality product is not budget-friendly (ironically, that's true most of the time). We can understand it this way: for many potential buyers, it is not the best product/solution. For example, when one talks about the best driving experience, we all visualise Mercedes or BMW. It is a given fact, but does it mean that everyone owns one? No. Why? Because despite being of the best quality, they are expensive. Therefore, many can't afford them and hence are not a good fit for their current needs or *not the best solution*. You need to buy a car for commuting but don't have the money to either buy a Mercedes or BMW; will you wait until the time you have the needed amount, or will you go for a cheaper option? Rationality says that, for the moment at least, go for the second-best alternative until you can afford your desired car. So, given the *constraint(s)*, Toyota or Honda is the best car for you, and a salesperson working in those companies should use the point to their advantage.

You see, being the best is very subjective (Messi and Ronaldo debate), and as a seller, one has to play around with this subjectivity factor. Again, I will go back to a point previously stated; we are dealing with people who have different needs and constraints, and each buyer should be tackled accordingly. One of the basic pillars of modern-day economics is the concept of scarcity, which says that people have unlimited needs (and wants) but have limited resources to fulfil them. Thus, they are forced to make certain *unfavourable choices*. And, if I may dare say, this is where we sellers try to *cash in*.

Back to the original discussion.

Next, ask them why you think your product/solution is the best. What makes you arrive at that conclusion? Majority will be silent or will give run-of-the-mill replies. This is because they have never attempted to sell the products to themselves, or should I say, have never tried to analyse from their customers' perspective. My point of view is that confidence in knowing your product/solution is the best should be based on rationality, where you have concrete arguments to prove your points. This way, you will be even more confident in front of your clients and can back up all your valid points based on handling customer objections with appropriate facts and figures. You are here working from your grounding, and you share with the prospect or potential buyer only what you know. This means you do not make-up stuff to embellish the product's attractiveness and do not talk down about your competitors. As they say: Do not tell your customer that the competitor's solution they are looking at is effectively an "ugly baby" in your eyes.

Secondly, and more importantly, critically analysing your product/solution will allow you to identify its USP (Unique Selling Point) better. I am not suggesting that companies don't know the USPs of their products. No, I am simply propounding that rather than being told about it by seniors, a seller should find it for themselves through their own understanding and personal assessment. As a salesperson, you will feel empowered since you will have ONE important factor to base your arguments around and impress upon the customers the need, and the reason, to buy the product/solution. If you can handle the how (*how can your product satisfy my needs?*) and why (*why should I buy your product?*) of the purchasers satisfactorily, nothing can stop you from securing the deal.

Don't Just Meet the Targets; Blast Through Them

This is more important for youngsters who have less than five years of experience. I know seniors will give you monthly or quarterly sales targets but set your goals higher than the official figures. Your aim should be to achieve your personally determined mark; keep the ones communicated by the team leader, or the manager, aside, don't think about it too much. The practice will serve dual purposes; one, you will have more confidence in your judgements and will feel encouraged to make your decisions.

Secondly, it will provide a cushion. During your professional career, there will be a phase where you will not be able to perform at your best. It has happened to the best of us and can happen to anybody. After all, we all are human and have a life apart from our profession. Any untoward event in our personal lives can directly impact our performance. Though it is not desirable, but practically speaking, it is something that can't be avoided. Hence, if you have a history of consistently performing better than management's expectations, that bad phase will not impact your overall results that much.

Many times, sellers limit themselves to the communicated sales targets and don't think beyond those figures. This habit can prove to be detrimental in the long run. As a person, you get used to spoon-feeding - being told every time what to do rather than deciding for yourself - which is not a great attribute to have if you want to climb up the organisational ladder. After a certain period of time, top management expects a professional to start making their own decisions. If someone is not doing that, it places a huge question mark over their ability to progress ahead and take on a leadership role. I have seen experienced people struggling with making simple decisions throughout my professional career despite being brilliant in their fields. Consequently, they have been limited to a certain role that doesn't offer much professional growth. So, don't confine yourselves; don't anchor down when you can sail ahead.

Get out of your comfort zone and explore the world. Remember, the more you explore, the more you know, and the more you can contribute. And, no organisation can say no to anyone who has been producing more than had been asked for. My suggestion to young aspirants will be to treat the official sales targets as the *starting point*; the bare minimum you have to achieve but remember: not even the sky is the limit here. You have infinite options to succeed. Only your limiting beliefs could keep you down and again you can work on those when you realise that your confidence comes from your innate state/ from within you.

Don't Assume, Act!

The English cricket team example I shared earlier fits perfectly here. The team management decided not to sit idle and go for the results and have come up with trumps.

The same logic applies to every professional, especially the sellers.

There is a beautiful quote, I read it somewhere but unfortunately can't recall where that "ifs" and "buts" don't count in real life. How true is that! If a person gets into this habit of daydreaming state where they keep telling themselves: if this happens, then I can achieve that, or if that happens, then I can do that; you know that they will not go anywhere, nor will they achieve anything. Try to understand one thing, planning is good, and everyone should plan for a better future. However, results will not come by themselves; one has to go out and execute those plans to realise the goals. Had mere planning been enough, there was no need to work; everyone would have been a millionaire by now, am I right?

Based on my experience, I am advising young sales professionals the following: don't think that since you are a part of a great team and/or an organisation, everything will fall into place by itself. No, you will need to put in your efforts; there is no shortcut to success.

Similarly, I have observed recently that sales professionals are relying more and more on marketing, and the brand value of their respective products/services, to help them achieve their targets. This is a dangerous proposition. The job of marketing is not to get you sales; they are there to a) create brand awareness, b) educate customers about the benefits of using their products/services, and c) generate leads. Sellers have to perform their duties efficiently if they want their incentives; there is no free lunch out there. More importantly, what you want to achieve; a free rider is not welcome anywhere.

Ask any prominent sales expert, and you will know how much effort they all must put in to reach where they are now. Yes, after gaining some experience, one can differentiate between hard work and smart work, but you need relevant working experience. Remember, only those who reach for the stars will get there. Please never limit yourself as your true potential is limitless!

Give Yourself Some Margin of Error

Time to relax, grab a drink or a coffee and let go of your worries. Don't stress out if things don't go your way momentarily. It is important not to allow bad and negative thoughts get to your head because it will adversely affect your performance even more. I have yet to meet someone achieving great results by overthinking or stressing out.

We all talk about being motivated, fronting up to the challenges, and staying strong. However, it can never be sustained all the time. As humans, we all have an emotional side, and at times things do go bad, really bad, resulting in a feeling of remorse. However, it is more important to bounce back from that low point, like a phoenix rising from its own ashes.

One of the important things I learned from my seniors is to *own your failures just like you own your success*. It may sound absurd initially, but it holds the key to success. There is no harm in admitting one's mistakes. No one is infallible here; even the best in the business make mistakes, so there is no point hiding yours. However, how you mend your ways and come back is what defines your true character and how strong a warrior you are. Also, don't forget that not admitting your mistake will only hurt you more because then you will not be able to find a solution or a way out of the created mess. A person living in denial can never find the right path because he has not admitted that he is on the wrong path in the first place.

So, my advice will be as long as you have committed an honest mistake, don't feel too bad about it. Instead, take it as a learning experience. Just like Edison, who once famously said, "I have not failed 10,000 times—I've successfully found 10,000 ways that will not work" (Gates, 2016).

Ω

Chapter Five: Know Your Buyer

Let's now talk about the person sitting at the other side of the table. For sellers, he/she is the most important individual in the company since they must decide whether to buy or reject a product. However, despite the significance, most salespersons tend to overlook researching about their clients; hence, the title *Know Your Buyer*.

Stephen Elop, CEO of Nokia Corporation, in 2014, after announcing the acquisition of Nokia by Microsoft, famously said, "we didn't do anything wrong, but somehow, we lost" (Gupta, 2016). If you haven't taken your customers seriously before, time to wake up now.

For those who don't know, Nokia was a giant in the mobile phone industry before Samsung and Apple. Ask any old-timer, and they will tell you about the company and what it meant to its customers. Nokia mobiles were known for their durability, excellent performance, and long battery backup. It was nothing short of a privilege to use them. However, for unknown reasons, the company shut its doors to all the innovations, relying instead on its age-old keypad models to keep delivering the goods. The move backfired, though.

Despite being the industry leader, Nokia's management failed to recognise that Apple, Samsung, and Blackberry had been launching mobiles that offered more than just texting and calling services. Added features of these sets lured the customers away as their priorities altered from durability and long battery backup to sleek designs, chic looks, and touchscreen operations. Nokia's *stubbornness* in not being able to comprehend the changing buyer behaviour led to its fall from grace and the eventual takeover by Microsoft. Those who don't value their customers are bound to fail because buyers wait for no one, especially in the present day and age when there are hundreds of competitive products on the market.

So, what does it mean to know your buyer?

To accomplish this task, sellers have to ask themselves the following questions:

- Why does a person buy a product?
- What problem will the product/solution solve for the buyer?
- How do they buy?
- Type of buyer – individual or corporate?
- Do they buy themselves or rely on others?
- What importance does the product hold for them?
- What is their lifestyle?
- Why should he buy my product? What value are we offering?

Coming up with appropriate answers to the above questions allows a company to create what marketing people call a *buyer persona*. "The buyer persona is a semi-fictional representation of your ideal customers based on data and research. They help you focus your time on qualified prospects, guide product development to suit the needs of your target customers, and align all work across your organisation (from marketing to sales to service)" (Vaughan, 2022).

Chapter Five: Know Your Buyer

As discussed earlier, a commercial organisation's primary reason for coming into being is to satisfy the needs of its customers. Businesses aim to provide the best possible solutions to their clients to grow and succeed. For this to happen, it is imperative that the management knows beforehand about the needs of its prospective customers, their buying behaviour, and their grievances, if any, from other products. Combining the replies to all such questions helps the organisation to create a wholesome product, identify and target the appropriate audience better, and be able to communicate with them appropriately.

Though the image being created of the buyer is hypothetical in nature, it still serves more than one purpose. It provides direction to the marketing and sales campaigns, acting as a launch pad for the brand's identity and placement, and lastly, provides connectivity with the customer. Among different messages, if a buyer finds one which addresses his needs and is crisp, he will most certainly go for the product/solution. The message will hook him up until he utilises the item, after which a more informed decision can be made. However, by that time, the company has achieved its target of enticing the customer and making him buy the product/solution.

How to Create the Brand Persona

Collect first-hand information from the customers. Usually, companies engage third-party surveyors for such practices.

Next, segment the responses according to the type of respondents and their replies. Industry type and job titles of the respondents can also be used in the segmentation process. This practice will help you zero in to create a near-perfect picture of your prospective buyer, which will help you decide about the marketing and sales offers.

Lastly, make use of your competitors' data and position in the market. Which segments are they more active in? What is the reason behind their success? And why a certain type of people like their products?

Using this information will allow a company to come up with a specific buyer persona that they intend to target through their products/services.

Ω

Chapter Six: Competition

You might have noticed that as we continue our journey towards identifying and adopting the best-selling practices (and techniques) to make a great career in the profession, our scope and canvas are enlarging. From a personal and an individual seller's perspective, we are now entering the strategic realm. We will intermittently touch upon topics like team management, which is a supervisory role and includes multiple personalities. The progression replicates the career paths of sales professionals as they work their way up the organisational ladder. Though the book is about guiding individuals, the *management part* can't be ignored altogether. After all, that's what we all desire. So, brace yourself for donning the manager's hat if you haven't reached that stage yet in your real life. We are providing you with the opportunity early to plan ahead; you are welcome ☺.

For any professional, more so a seller, there are two kinds of competition: intra-organisational, from your peers and teammates, and inter-organisational, from the professionals of other companies working in the same field. Both are essential for growth and should be carefully monitored all the time. Like organisations, a person should also know about their competitors, their performances, reasons behind success, and shortcomings to chart out a plan of their own. Those who overlook these important realities are often left behind and end up always playing a catching game. They can only *react* to the events happening around them instead of controlling them.

Rise High Among the Team Members

The ultimate truth of life: it is lonely being at the top! What does it mean? As you grow professionally, opportunities will decrease until a person reaches a point where he sits alone at the top of the ladder. Business management seems to have borrowed the idea from the military's *Unity of Command* concept, which

Chapter Six: Competition

means a specific task or operation, should be led by one person or commander (Strain, 2007). Thus, every organisation, whether they follow a vertical or horizontal structure, looks like a pyramid; more people at the base, only one at the top.

Look around in your company; there may be fifty sales representatives, but only ten team leaders looking after them. Go one step further, and those ten team leaders are under four sales managers, who in turn are under two senior managers, and at the top is the *lonely figure* of the head of the sales department. Observe the exponential decrease in the number of people as the stakes increase. What does it imply for young professionals? Survival of the fittest. If you want to reach the top, be prepared to grind out through all the challenges life has to throw at you. And let me tell you, these challenges will come from all directions; right, left, and centre, simply from everywhere. Secondly, and more importantly, you must let go of your friends who do not encourage and support you in pursuit of your goals. Find yourself a mentor, someone who has done this journey before you and can guide you. Remember, only ONE will reach the summit; it's either one of them or you. Not all of you can be head of sales in a company. Clash of interests? Personal dilemma... *feeling nervous...?*

That's what people, in general, talk about. For them, success can't be achieved without stepping over others, like on a battlefield where victory can only be guaranteed after killing and bloodshed. Hence over the years, words like cutthroat have been used to define competition.

However, my approach is different; I believe in the *Blue Ocean Theory* (Freedman, 2023). It is "the simultaneous pursuit of high product differentiation and low cost, making the competition irrelevant." Keywords are: *pursuit of high product differentiation* and *making the competition irrelevant.* This theory has presented to me another view of competition: no competition. Improve your skills and performance to such an extent that no one can compete with you. The ideology may seem difficult to follow, but it will clear your way towards success. A consistent performer can't be denied for long. It is a universal truth and works in every aspect of life.

Let me give you an example. Sachin Tendulkar, one of the greatest batters of all time, played cricket for twenty years. He holds all the imaginable batting records. His

Chapter Six: Competition

mantra was very simple: *let the bat do the talking*. Despite being a godly figure in India, he maintained a low profile throughout his playing days; no showboating, no boastful claims or interviews, absolutely nothing. Two decades of professional cricket, and he wasn't involved in any off-the-field controversies. Why? For him, the cricket field was the best place to reply to all his critics and naysayers. Result: whole of the cricketing world adores him, while his nation worships him. He took himself to such high levels that every competition paled in front of him. It has been more than eleven years since his retirement, but still, his greatness is admired.

We can learn a lot from the *Master Blaster*. Remain humble and grounded, despite all the accolades, and never lose your focus, no matter what others say. Concentrate on your target all the time, and keep planning ways to achieve it. The rumour mills will die down naturally if you keep on producing results. Now the big question is how to do it? (Gallo et al., 2021), (Petrone, 2022).

Build a Good Rapport with Team Members

I can sense an element of surprise; well, you are not alone. Many others reacted the same way when I shared the tip with them. One of the oldest myths of sales is the *Lone Wolf Seller* myth. I say myth because, in reality, wolves hunt in a pack. They like to stick around under their leader through thick and thin. Thus, whoever came up with this idea didn't know anything about wolves and sales.

There doesn't exist any proverbial super-seller who can turn around a company on his own. This has never happened before and most probably will never happen in the future. Sales is all about teamwork. As discussed earlier, meeting people with different personalities and needs and replying to their queries satisfactorily is not an easy task. It requires group planning and information sharing. Yes, as a salesperson, you need to cater to your customers. However, discussing the modalities of a sales call with respect to a specific buyer with teammates can only prove beneficial. Try to create a congenial atmosphere where team members can give honest feedback. Remember, you can't rely on your team leader or manager for everything. As a professional, you also need to take some initiative, and the practice will bode well for the future.

Demonstrate Strategical Skills

Most men don't want to step out of their comfort zones. They want to remain in the pre-defined domain, preferring status quo over change, since coming out of it will open up new challenges. They view the situation with a negative mindset, equating challenges to problems. However, challenges should be viewed as new opportunities to learn and grow. The famous Chinese war strategist Sun Tzu, in his greatest literary work, *The Art of War*, wrote, *"In the midst of chaos, there is also opportunity."* How true is that? We have always been taught that opportunities and problems are two sides of the same coin, then why people don't trust this general wisdom?

Experience is the greatest teacher. It opens new avenues of getting things right and guides you how to come out of tough situations. However, if you are not willing to experience something new, how will you learn? How will you test your capabilities if you shy away from challenging tasks? Inactivity means death of learning and hence growth. Even water, considered a source of life, loses its vitality once it stagnates and requires constant cleaning. So why not live like a stream, constantly flowing ahead, brimming with new ideas, and taking on challenges head-on?

My dear readers, don't be afraid of discussing new ideas with your managers. However, back your claims with concrete data. No need to shoot arrows in the air; one may come down to hurt you. Think beyond your job description and show the willingness to take on greater responsibilities. One word of caution: don't just do it to impress your senior, do it for your own personal sake, to learn and grow. Contrary to the general perception, many managers like to see individuals taking the initiative and view them favourably.

Outside Competition

Now we will turn our attention towards outside-the-organisation competition. Here you are up against the companies, and their sales representatives, vying to woo your customers away to increase/strengthen their hold on the market. This is where the individual part ends, and the cumulative part begins, as mentioned at the start of the chapter. While dealing with the outside competition, as a seller, you are not a separate entity but a representative of your company. So, by extension, your company is your identity. Before discussing the competition further, it is better to mention its different types (Radosavljevic, 2022), (Rodrigue, 2022).

Direct Competitor

If a company is producing the same product or offering the same services as your company, then it is classified as a direct competitor. It is the most obvious of all the competitors and the one which requires most planning.

Indirect Competitor

If a company is not producing the same product or offering the same services as yours, but is operating in the same domain or field, then it is classified as an indirect competitor.

Replacement Competitor

A company not operating in the same field as yours but is offering products/services which can be consumed or availed by the same customers, then it is classified as a replacement competitor.

I know some of you might be confused between the indirect competitor and replacement competitor or whether a replacement competitor can be termed as genuine, so let me just clarify through examples.

Scenario# 1: You have had a hectic week and want to enjoy your weekend watching some quality football. You go through the Premier League schedule and find out that on Saturday evening, there will be a Manchester derby between United and City and a London derby between Arsenal and Spurs. Two matches you love, but both starting at the same time. That's direct competition, where Manchester and London derbies are direct competitors of each other.

Scenario# 2: It is a bright August Saturday afternoon, and you want to enjoy it by watching quality live sports. You switch on your TV to find out that on one channel is the London derby, while on another is the last day of the fourth Ashes test, with the series hanging on line. This is indirect competition because cricket and football are two different sports, but they cater to the same need.

Chapter Six: Competition

Scenario# 3: It is Saturday evening, and you are free. So, you decided to watch the London derby at the Emirates Stadium. However, just as you are about to confirm your tickets, you receive a call from your friend informing you about an Ed Shereen concert. Furthermore, he tells you that he has tickets available, though not for free, and forces you to join him. The two events are replacement competitors because they belong to different fields altogether; however, they can only be *consumed* separately. You either have to attend the concert or watch the match. Thus, they replace each other.

From the above examples, you can make out that replacement competitors are the most difficult to deduct because practically no one knows for sure about customers' buying behaviour. This occurs more with FMCG, where consumer decision-making varies more and may not necessarily follow a general trend. Thus, sellers of over-the-counter consumables in this regard have more to think about regarding their sales strategy and campaigns.

Counter Strategy

This is the ultimate dream of any seller, devising a successful counter-strategy to see off the competition. It can happen at any point, either personal and tactical level or organisational and strategic level. One important to add; although a sales strategy is handed down from the top, it generally is the amalgamation of the sales teams' feedback. Thus, as I have mentioned before, never shy away from sharing any important piece of information which you might have observed and experienced from your team leaders and managers. Such inputs and pieces of advice can make a difference while coming up with the perfect sales strategy.

Now that we have identified the competition, the next logical step is to counter it. Some would use the term creating a barrier between yourself and your competitors.

Be Proactively Consistent

Henry Ford, the founder of the Ford Motor Company, was a visionary businessman who revolutionised the automobile industry forever. He is also credited for helping America become the economic superpower in the early twentieth century, but that's beyond our scope.

Henry Ford launched his company in 1903. In those days, there was no concept of mass production; every car used to be custom-made with unique designs and colours, hence, was very expensive and had considerable lead time. In a bid to outwit his existing competitors, Ford came up with the idea of a standard-design car, offering great performance at relatively lower prices. The move clicked, and the company's revenues grew exponentially in the initial years.

After a decade, in 1913, Ford introduced the idea of *moving assembly line*. It further reduced the lead time and production cost. Even after a hundred years, all automobile companies follow the moving assembly line concept (Editors, 2019).

By proactively consistent, I mean providing customers with what they want even before they ask for it. Ford realised the demand for cars and also recognised that customization was the greatest hurdle since the practice was making the product expensive, making it out of the reach of the common man. Thus, he came up with a novel concept and swept through the market.

More importantly, the company remained consistent with this approach of coming up with new ideas. Hence even today, it is the second-biggest automobile manufacturer in the U.S., behind only General Motors (Anand, 2023).

If you are thinking, how is it possible? Talk to your customers and learn more about their needs. Sometimes, people find it difficult to explicitly put forward their requirements, so learn to read between the lines and decipher the meaning. Again, this usually happens in consumer/individual buying; corporate buyers are more assured about their requirements and, hence, know the products/services they need. However, one thing that even corporate customers value is consistency, both in product quality and customer service.

Learn from Competitors

"If you know the enemy and know yourself, you need not fear the result of a hundred battles. If you know yourself but not the enemy, for every victory gained you will also suffer a defeat. If you know neither the enemy nor yourself, you will succumb in every battle."

Sun Tzu, Art of War.

Chapter Six: Competition

The above quote, my dear readers, encapsulates the whole business strategy. If sellers don't know how their competitors are performing, then they will never survive. By performing, I mean learning about their products and examining their pros and cons. Why are customers buying their products and not yours? Are customers more satisfied with their products? If yes, then how are competitors' solutions fulfilling their needs better? What are the deficiencies of their products which your company can work upon?

Asking yourself these questions and doing a little bit of reverse engineering will give salespersons all the answers they need to a) present their products better to customers and b) provide better feedback to the product management team to consider enhancements/ additional features etc. Such insightful suggestions also count as the productivity of a seller; thus, I repeat, never undermine the value of genuine and honest feedback. However, it should be backed up with facts and accompanied by recommendations.

I will conclude by saying that learning demands patience and hard work. If you want to succeed, always consider yourself a student and keep updating your skill set. Don't try to fast-track the process, and never get disheartened by the failures. These mistakes teach us more. Nothing comes easy in life; you must earn it. Don't forget, enjoy the actual journey and once you achieve your goal, nothing can be sweeter than that feeling.

Ω

Chapter Seven: You Can Do It, Provided You Want To!

As the curtain falls on 2022, we also reach the end of this book. *How fast the night changes!*

In one of his books, *Sell or Be Sold*, Grant Cardone has explained the evolution of a salesperson from an amateur to a professional level. He has highlighted certain factors which, according to him, make or break a seller's career. In this chapter, we will be discussing those with some personal insight.

Commitment

Sales is the only profession that comes naturally to every human being. It is applicable in every sphere of life; even professionals from other fields can't survive the market competition without possessing good selling skills. Remember, in the opening chapter, we discussed how everyone uses sales to their advantage. The only difference being the non-monetary nature of their transactions.

Though it is a universal phenomenon, commitment has extra value in sales. Continuous travelling, meeting different people, and listening to their queries and complaints, can be challenging for any individual. And if you are new to sales and are not used to rejections, that's the cherry on top. These factors have all the potential to derail an individual's sales career, forcing him to switch professions. This is where commitment comes in and plays its part. Devoting oneself to achieving the goals propels a person forward. It overlooks the temporary failures and keeps focusing on the larger picture. A fully committed person is always clear in his mind and knows what to do and when to do it. Additionally, he will take the opportunity to create a better space for himself to progress.

Humans Over Products/Services

What sets sales apart from other professions is its human element, which sometimes gets lost on the higher management and the professionals. More often, sellers equip themselves with product knowledge without focusing on the person sitting on the other end - the customer. Ask him what he needs and why he needs it. These should be the two basic premises around which the whole conversation should revolve. Get your customers to talk more so you can gather as much information as possible. It will help you in presenting your product in accordance with their needs.

Learn to respect your customers. Don't treat them with contempt, someone who could be manipulated into buying your product. This approach can never guarantee long-term success. Instead, lend an ear to them and listen to their concerns. Let them feel you are there to solve their problems and help them make better choices.

A Bird in Hand is Worth Two in The Bush

While it is perfectly fine to search for new clients, never lose sight of your existing ones. Keep following up with them at regular intervals to make them feel valued and respected. Having a long-lasting relationship with your buyers is a recipe for great success. Many sellers ignore the importance of looking after existing customers and pay a heavy price. If you have satisfied customers, then you can be assured of positive feedback and organic marketing through word of mouth. Most buyers, like other professionals, are connected and value each other's advice. If your customer talks favourably about you in the group, it will surely attract their attention, which may result in sales. Imagine having a person doing your job for free. However, for that, you have to build a strong rapport with the customers by honouring your commitments, regular follow-ups, and delivering high-quality products.

These three factors may look simple, but even experienced professionals stumble upon them. There is no rocket science attached to sales. It is all about common sense and emotional intelligence. According to the Harvard Business School website, *emotional intelligence - also known as EQ - is defined as the ability to understand and manage your own emotions, as well as recognise and influence the emotions of those around you* (Landry, 2019). EQ allows an individual to communicate positively with others with the ability to achieve desired results in the end. All effective leaders are known to have high EQ, empowering them to influence their peers and subordinates into following their vision.

The article singled out the leadership trait with high EQ. However, I believe it is also necessary to achieve success as a seller. We deal with different personalities throughout the year. They all have different needs, workplace pressure, and working style. In order to assimilate and *decode* their messages effectively, one needs to be calm and emotionally stable. Secondly, he should be able to read between the lines to *infer* the correct meanings. The ability to see through a buyer's thought process through a simple conversation between one human being to another and identify what your buyer actually desires. Then present products/services to your client as the best solution for the problem and close the deal.

One important thing to note here is that EQ is not a God-gifted talent. It is a combination of skills that anyone can master and use to their advantage.

Self-Awareness

The first step to a great career is to be mindful of one's own strengths, weaknesses, and emotional well-being. By emotional well-being, I mean the ability to remain calm under stress. Workplace pressure is a given thing; one can't entirely avoid it. Accordingly, for a professional, it is important to rein in their emotions and avoid overreacting to any situation, as it may count negatively against them. In every stressful or seemingly unsolvable problem, you need to stay calm and draw on your inner resources to find a way to resolve any given issue. Even five to ten minutes away from the desk, outside in the fresh air, can do miracles in terms of refreshed focus which inadvertently leads to a new outlook and positive generation of new ideas.

Self-Management

A self-aware person can manage their emotions really well as they pace themselves and do not need to react to a situation immediately. Here self-management is about maintaining a positive demeanour despite adversities and avoiding knee-jerk reactions to any negative or unwanted news. Self-managed people always pause for a bit to recollect their thoughts before reacting to ensure they don't give away any negative signals to the audience. Your every move is being observed and plays a pivotal role in how the other party will judge you. If a buyer senses that you are a fidgety person who can panic under pressure, they will find it hard to trust you to deliver the goods. Don't forget; in their eyes, you are the image of the company you represent.

Social Awareness

The third step towards achieving high EQ is being socially aware. Sellers who are aware of the emotional condition of their buyers can even modify their message at the last minute to hit the right nerve with the customers. Empathy, or showing concern, in finding the perfect solution to their problem can get sellers to build long-lasting relationships with their customers. They view them as trustworthy and reliable and are comfortable working with them.

Relationship Management

This is the last stage, where a seller can influence others around him. Relationship management is the logical extension of social awareness. As a seller, you must understand that the buyer is also under pressure from other departments to source the material at the earliest. Hence, they try to shift the pressure to you by showing urgency. If you panic at this stage, you will lose the deal. Just make the buyer feel comfortable that their desired product will be available at their convenience.

This is how emotional intelligence, EQ, can benefit you in securing and closing out deals. From my experience, I can say that sometimes we lose out on sales not because of the product but because of how we communicate with the buyer and due to our body language. Remember what we have said earlier; we are dealing with humans, not robots or machines. This is why everything matters when trying to convince a buyer about our offering. There is a saying in sales that your whole body should communicate with the buyer. What does it mean? It means that you are so honestly committed to the work that you actually believe in it. That trust transfers positive vibes to the listener, buyer, and makes him think positively about you and your product/service.

Chapter 7: You Can Do It, Provided You Want To!

Consider yourself being a buyer for a moment. What will happen if you meet a person, who claims to be a seller, comes to you, and starts telling you about his product/services without any conviction? You will listen for a moment or two and then will lose focus. Why? Because you can feel that the person selling the product is not most importantly convinced himself. He is there just for the sake of it. Many of the deals don't materialise simply because of this factor.

On the other hand, if you meet a person who is passionate about their product and is enthusiastic about finding you a suitable solution, you would at least listen carefully to what he is trying to convey to you. It is all about attitude. Only those who possess the right attitude will succeed. Here attitude means looking forward to making a difference, being the game changer, and being a problem solver. Any sales expert/writer you listen to or read will only talk about this one thing. Yes, you as a seller need to get to the nitty-gritty part of sales, but that's secondary. First, you need to develop the right approach and most importantly the right mindset. You can't build a strong building without a solid foundation; having the right attitude is that solid foundation that will ensure a long and successful career in sales.

Ω

Chapter Eight: Rise of the Phoenix - Kohli

If the 1990s and 2000s were about Tendulkar and Ricky Ponting, respectively, then the 2010s were about Virat Kohli. Some may argue about Hashim Amla and AB de Villiers, but their dominance was short-lived and limited; Virat's impact has been all-encompassing. The Dehli-born batter has the talent and the aura, the swag, which elevates him above his peers. In that sense, Kohli resembles Sir Viv Richards; you can feel his presence on the ground and the vibe he generates. Virat exemplifies the true character of the modern-day cricketer: talented, vocal (wearing his emotions on his sleeve), and fitness conscious. As a cricket lover, I can safely say he is one player one would not mind performing against their own team, provided the result is favourable.

Kohli took on the mantle of his side's ace batter after Tendulkar's retirement in 2011 and probably had the best mentor a young player could ask for, MS Dhoni – Captain Cool. Though Virat's talent was obvious, he didn't have a canter at the international level, with England, New Zealand, and South Africa proving too hard to conquer. Those who follow cricket know that for Asian batters SENA countries (South Africa, England, New Zealand, and Australia) offer the toughest challenge due to the swing and seam movements and the extra bounce off the pitch. Though Australia was conquered immediately, *King Kohli* initially found it hard to score runs in England and New Zealand. He had to make adjustments in stance and batting technique to eventually come good.

By 2016, Virat Kohli reached the zenith of his career and managed to remain there until 2019. Three years of absolute mayhem, if you are at the receiving end, but an unimaginable joy for Indians and neutrals. As an unbiased sports lover, one can't help but admire his flair and exuberance. He was winning matches for his team left, right, and centre; in my humble opinion, Kohli was the first batter to rule all three formats simultaneously. During that period, in Rob Palmer's parlance, *we witnessed the best batter at the absolute peak of his powers*[2]. Such was his dominance that ICC awarded him the Player of the Decade award in 2020, while Nasser Hussain, an ex-English captain and a renowned commentator, dubbed him the *Chase Slayer*; for Kohli, no total was too big.

Kohli juggernaut went on unchecked for three years till 22 Nov 2019. India was playing a test series against Bangladesh, and on this day, he scored his 70th international hundred, placing him third among the all-time leading international century scorers. Considering that he was only 31, everyone was waiting for the day when he would eventually surpass Tendulkar's record of 100 international centuries; it looked a mere formality. But then the unimaginable happened. All of a sudden, centuries stopped for the run-machine Kohli, who used to score them for fun. Initially, fatigue and workload were identified as the main factors that prompted him to

---

[2] During commentary, Rob Palmer once praised Messi as, "We are witnessing possibly the greatest player ever at the absolute peak of his powers."

start skipping some of the less important matches. But the drought wouldn't end.

Being a cricketing star in India has its pros and cons; a player is worshipped and vilified all at the same time. Furthermore, if he happens to be the captain, pressure multiplies manifold; it is a double-edged sword that can cut the opponent as well as the holder/owner. Soon dissenting voices begin to surface. Though Kohli was consistently piling up runs, his failure to convert those scores into centuries allowed the naysayers to keep blowing their trumpets. *Suggestions* like giving young blood more chances, especially in white-ball cricket, made the headlines. India's favourite son was not everyone's blue-eyed boy anymore, and it showed in his demeanour.

However, there was a ray of hope.

Australia was supposed to host the T20 world cup in Nov 2020, but a Covid outbreak saw hosting rights transferred to India. The tournament was eventually played out in UAE in 2021. Still playing in familiar conditions afforded Kohli, and his team, a great advantage. With a star-packed batting line-up, the men-in-blue were the clear favourites. To spice up the matters, the first match was against Pakistan – the arch-rivals and a team India hasn't lost against in any of their world cup fixtures, either 50 or 20-over format.

While Kohli was struggling to convert his starts into something substantial, a young batter across the border started making headlines. Renowned as a land of pacers, Pakistan, for once, has produced a world-class batter who was taking the world by storm. With centuries in different parts of the world and across the formats, a certain Babar Azam was lying a claim to the throne of the cricketing world. Therefore, the world cup match was dubbed the Kohli vs. Babar show; the King vs. the Heir-apparent, with over a billion eyes watching.

24 Oct 2021 can be termed as one of the lowest points of Kohli's international career, if not the lowest. His team lost the match to a resurgent Pakistan team, which drew a lot of flak from their supporters. Eventually, India failed to go past the group stage. The disappointment of failing in home-like conditions meant condemnation and stripping of captaincy. Kohli, the biggest asset of the Indian cricket team, suddenly became a liability and there were calls for his head. *How fast the night changes!*

Feeling overlooked, Kohli decided to take some time out from cricket to concentrate on his mental health. His absence further fuelled the rumours of him being shown the door by the Indian cricket board, especially in the T20 format.

Sept 2022, Sri Lanka hosted the T20-format Asia Cup in UAE due to its worsening political condition. Kohli made a comeback in the Indian line-up and demonstrated some flashes of his past brilliance. During press conferences, he talked at length about mental peace and being in harmony with himself. Though India failed to qualify for the finals, Kohli was the tournament's leading scorer after scoring his first T20I century. The century jinx was broken, and it was just the beginning.

Oct 2022, Australia hosted the T20 world cup to compensate for the loss during the Covid. India and Pakistan were in the same group and, like the previous world cup, were supposed to open their tournament against each other. However, this time the tables were turned; due to Bumrah's absence and Pakistan's strong fast bowling, India was not considered the favourites. Crescendo built again!

Pakistan, despite Babar's failure and tough batting conditions, scored enough to test the Indians. And they did exactly that. Chasing 160, the Indian team were 31 for the loss of 4 wickets after 6.1 overs; Virat was at the crease with Pandya. Time for Kohli the Chase Slayer to step up and remind the world of his class. Slowly but surely, he built a partnership and then, at the end, launched a scathing attack that even the bowling line-up with the likes of Shaheen Afridi and Haris Rauf couldn't control. India won the match in the last over, with Virat going unbeaten for 82.

Redemption!

The outpouring of emotions by Kohli showed what it meant to him. It also reaffirmed his stature as the rightful king of the cricketing world. Though he has strong competition in Babar Azam, for now, he retains his throne.

So, dear readers, what is the point of writing this whole story? Some of you who don't follow cricket might not know Kohli, whom I have been glorifying for so long. Well, yes, I do like him as a cricketer, but I wanted to show you the similarities between professional athletes and us. How?

- Kohli was a generational talent but needed a mentor to shine. Similarly, in our professional careers, we need a guide to show us the way. I would ask managers and team leaders to show more faith in their subordinates and let them prove their talent. Don't reject them for minute mistakes. Conversely, I would also like to ask young professionals to listen to their seniors and try to learn from their experience. There is no shortcut to experience, and certainly, no book can teach you better than an experienced professional who has been there and done that.
- Despite all the talent, keep yourself open for improvements like Kohli did to counter the swing and seam of English and Kiwi conditions. Always remember no one is perfect; the day you stop learning, your downfall will start. Master the nuances of your trade at the earliest so that you may climb up the fastest.
- Once you have hit the peak, try to stay there as long as possible through adaptability and hard work. Kohli, despite being the best player in the planet, continued working hard to improve his batting and fitness, and it helped him to maintain

his place at the top. So, don't doze off after tasting success because it will not take you long to come down, and in this cut-throat environment, you may not even get a second chance.

- Everything that goes up will come down; it is the undisputable law of nature. No one will stay at the top for eternity. Therefore, if for some reason things are not working out for you, don't stress yourselves. Give your best so that no one can blame you for not trying, but flow with the motion and don't try to dictate the terms. Eventually, results will come; just be patient and ride out the wave.
- You may also take some time out and free your mind from all the worries. Track down the reasons you selected sales as a profession initially and start anew.
- Lastly, don't run away from competition; embrace it. You are not the only salesperson on this planet; sooner rather than later, you will find a worthy challenger. Don't shoo it off; try to learn from it and improve yourself. Off late, Kohli has talked lavishly about Babar, which shows his graciousness. This will also allow him to

concentrate on his batting with an open mind. Similarly, if you find a young competitor, pick up whatever you can from him and focus on your work. Don't ever belittle competition because without it you will cease to grow.

Recommended Reading

Blogs

- 3 Types of Competitors to Watch (+ How to Find Them) (https://blog.hubspot.com/marketing/types-competitors-business)
- 4 Ways for Sales Pros to Stand Out to Their Boss and Peers (https://www.linkedin.com/business/sales/blog/real-sales/stand-out-to-your-boss-and-peers-in-sales)
- 5 Personality Traits of Top Sales Leaders (https://blog.hubspot.com/sales/the-personality-of-a-perfect-salesperson-infographic)
- 7 Qualities a Really Good Salesperson Must Have (https://www.avidlyagency.com/blog/7-qualities-of-a-good-salesperson)
- 14 Important Traits Successful Salespeople Share (https://www.businessnewsdaily.com/4173-personality-traits-successful-sales-people.html)
- My Competitiveness Was Hurting My Sales Team. Here's How I Realized It (https://hbr.org/2017/09/my-competitiveness-was-hurting-my-sales-team-heres-how-i-realized-it)

- The Top 13 Most Important Sales Skills (https://www.edapp.com/blog/the-top-10-most-important-sales-skills/)
- What is the Cost of Customer Acquisition vs Customer Retention? (https://www.linkedin.com/pulse/what-cost-customer-acquisition-vs-retention-ian-kingwill)
- Why Emotional Intelligence is Important in Leadership (https://online.hbs.edu/blog/post/emotional-intelligence-in-leadership)

Books

- Art of War by Sun Tzu
- Blue Ocean Strategy by Renée Mauborgne and W. Chan Kim
- Gap Selling by Keenan
- Neuromarketing – Understanding the Buy Button in Your Customer's Brain by Patrick Renvoise and Christophe Morin
- Sell or Be Sold by Grant Cardone
- To Sell Is Human: The Surprising Truth About Moving Others by Daniel Pink

Bibliography

Anand, S. (2023, March 1). Ford Success Story: History: Business model. StartupTalky. Retrieved March 1, 2023, from https://startuptalky.com/ford-success-story/

Alfred, L. (2020, May 8). 5 personality traits of top sales leaders. HubSpot Blog. Retrieved March 1, 2023, from https://blog.hubspot.com/sales/the-personality-of-a-perfect-salesperson-infographic

Bariuad, S. (2022, December 12). 10 communication skills examples: EdApp: The mobile LMS. EdApp. Retrieved March 1, 2023, from https://www.edapp.com/blog/communication-skills-examples/

Editors, B. (2019). Henry Ford Biography. Biography.com. Retrieved March 1, 2023, from https://www.biography.com/business-leaders/henry-ford

Freedman, M. (2023). 14 important traits of successful salespeople. Business News Daily. Retrieved March 1, 2023, from https://www.businessnewsdaily.com/4173-personality-traits-successful-sales-people.html

Freedman, M. (2023). What is Blue Ocean Strategy? Business News Daily. Retrieved March 1, 2023, from https://www.businessnewsdaily.com/5647-blue-ocean-strategy.html

Gallo, A., Maimon, A., & Ashkenas, R. (2021, August 31). My competitiveness was hurting my sales team. here's how I realized it. Harvard Business Review. Retrieved March 1, 2023, from https://hbr.org/2017/09/my-competitiveness-was-hurting-my-sales-team-heres-how-i-realized-it

Gates, B. and M. (2016, February 22). Two superpowers we wish we had. gatesnotes.com. Retrieved March 1, 2023, from https://www.gatesnotes.com/2016-Annual-Letter

Kingwill, I. (2015). What is the cost of customer acquisition vs customer retention? LinkedIn. Retrieved March 1, 2023, from https://www.linkedin.com/pulse/what-cost-customer-acquisition-vs-retention-ian-kingwill

Kwapong, N. G. (n.d.). 7 qualities a really good salesperson must have. Avidly. Retrieved March 1, 2023, from https://www.avidlyagency.com/blog/7-qualities-of-a-good-salesperson

Landry, L. (2019, April 3). Emotional intelligence in leadership: Why it's important. Business Insights Blog. Retrieved March 1, 2023, from https://online.hbs.edu/blog/post/emotional-intelligence-in-leadership

Pink, D. (2018) To sell is human: the surprising truth about persuading, convincing and influencing others. Edinburgh: Canongate Books.

Petrone, P. (2022). 4 ways for sales pros to stand out to their boss and peers. LinkedIn. Retrieved March 1, 2023, from https://www.linkedin.com/business/sales/blog/real-sales/stand-out-to-your-boss-and-peers-in-sales

Rodrigue, E. (2022, January 20). 3 types of competitors to watch (+ how to find them). HubSpot Blog. Retrieved March 1, 2023, from https://blog.hubspot.com/marketing/types-competitors-business

Strain, J. (2007, August 16). Unity of command still important principle. > Joint Base Charleston > Display. Retrieved March 1, 2023, from https://www.jbcharleston.jb.mil/News/Commentaries/Display/Article/238522/unity-of-command-still-important-principle/

Vaughan, P. (2022, October 14). How to create detailed buyer personas for your business [free persona template]. HubSpot Blog. Retrieved March 1, 2023, from https://blog.hubspot.com/marketing/buyer-persona-research

www.ingramcontent.com/pod-product-compliance
Lightning Source LLC
Chambersburg PA
CBHW052156110526
44591CB00012B/1974